The Book of Duas
Translated
Phrase by Phrase
For Better Understanding
And
Easy Memorization

Dr. Muddassir Khan

Copyright © 2021

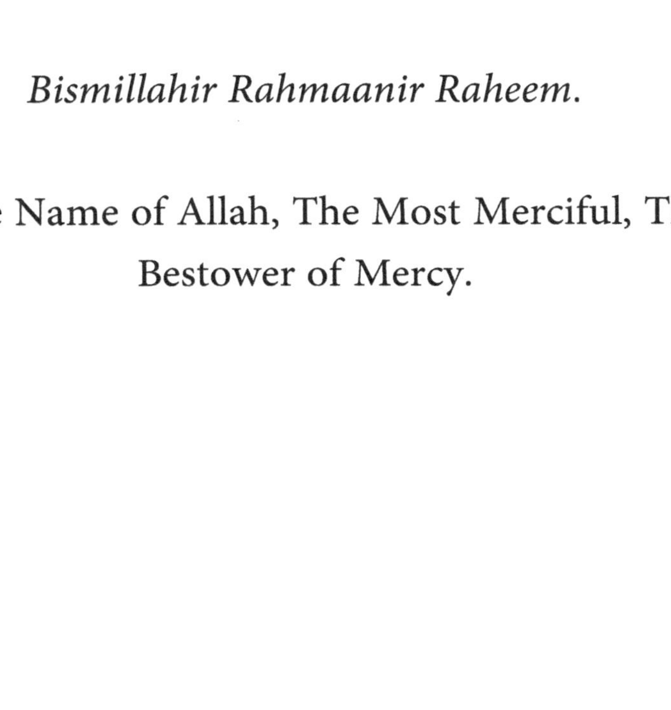

Bismillahir Rahmaanir Raheem.

In the Name of Allah, The Most Merciful, The Bestower of Mercy.

Table of Contents

When Waking Up 1

Before Entering The Toilet 11

When Starting Ablution 14

After Completing The Ablution 15

After Leaving The Toilet 20

Before Removing Clothes 21

After Wearing Clothes 22

After Wearing New Clothes 25

Supplication Said to Someone Who Is Wearing A New Garment

28

When Leaving The House

30

When Entering The House

35

On The Way To The Mosque

37

When Entering The Mosque

41

When Leaving The Mosque

43

Responding To the Adhan

45

Dua For Isthikharah (Seeking Allah's Help In Making A Decision)

53

Before Eating

63

After Eating

65

After Opening A Fast
....
70

When It Rains
....
72

Upon Hearing Thunder
....
73

Seeking Allah's protection for children
....
75

When Visiting The Sick
....
78

Supplication When Tragedy Strikes
....
82

What To Say When Consoling The Bereaved
....
85

Dua When Sighting The New Moon
....
87

Dua By The Guest For The Host
....
90

Dua If Someone Gives You Food Or Drink
....
92

Dua For The One Who Invites You To Break Your Fast With Them

94

What Should A Fasting Person Say When Abused

96

Dua Upon Seeing The First Fruits Of The Season

98

Dua After Sneezing

101

For Firmness Of The Heart

103

Dua To Congratulate Newly Weds

105

Dua By The Groom For His Wife, And When Purchasing A New Ride

107

Before Intercourse

110

Dua To Ward-off Anger

112

Dua On Seeing An Afflicted Person Or Upon Seeing Someone In Trial Or Tribulation

114

Dua While Sitting In A Gathering
....
117

Supplication For The Expiation Of Sins Said After a Sitting or a Gathering
....
119

Dua When Someone Seeks Forgiveness For You
....
121

Dua For The One Who Does You a Favour Or Who Does Good To You
....
123

Dua For The One Who Expresses His Love For Allah's Sake
....
125

Dua For The One Who Spends His Wealth On You
....
127

Dua When Repaying A Debt
....
129

Dua For Protection From Shirk
....
131

Dua For The One Who Prays For
....
134

Blessings For You

....
134

Dua Against Superstition and forbiddance of ascribing things to omens

....
136

Duaa When Riding A Vehicle Or An

....
138

Animal

....
138

Dua At The Start Of A Journey And On Return

....
142

Dua When Entering A Town Or City

....
149

What to say when entering a market

....
154

Du'a For When Your Vehicle Or Mount Gives Trouble or Stumbles

....
157

Dua By The Traveler For The Resident

....
159

The Morning And The Evening Adhkar

....
160

A Muslim is encouraged to utter certain phrases at the mention of Allah, the Prophet, other Prophets, the angels, the companions of the Prophet, and righteous Muslims. <u>Please say these phrases whenever you come across them in the book.</u>

Allah: Say *"Subhaanahuu wa ta'aalaa"* which means 'Glorified and Exalted is He.'

Prophet Muhammad: Say, *"Sallallaahu 'alayhi wa salam"* which means, 'May the peace and blessing of Allah be on him.' Say this phrase always when you hear the beloved name of the Prophet or at any place where the Prophet is mentioned.

Other Prophets or an Angel: Say, *"Alayhis Salaam"* which means, 'Peace be on him.'

A male companion of the Prophet: Say, "*Radiyallaahu 'anhum*" which means, 'May Allah be pleased with him.'

A past scholar or righteous Muslim: Say, "*Rahimahullaah*" which means, 'May Allah have Mercy on him.'

A female companion: Say "*Radiyallaahu 'anhaa*" which means, 'May Allah be pleased with her.'

When Waking Up

<u>Prayer 1</u>

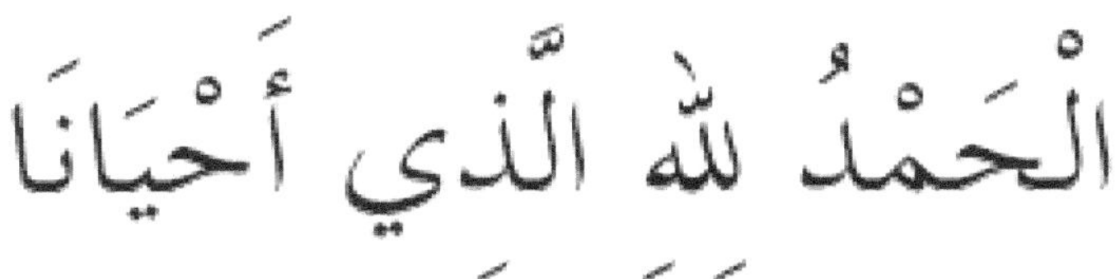

Praise be to Allah Who has given us life

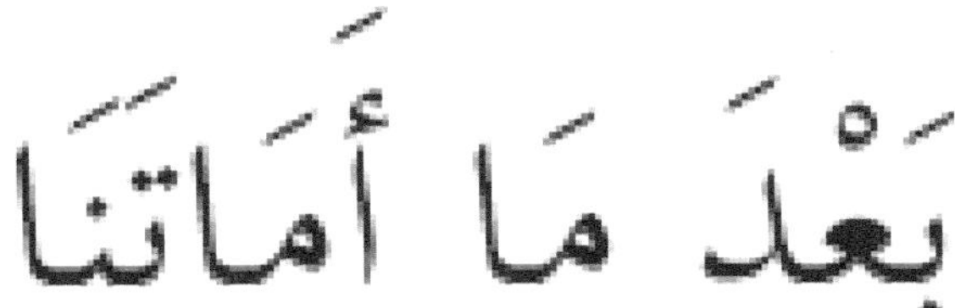

After He had caused us to die

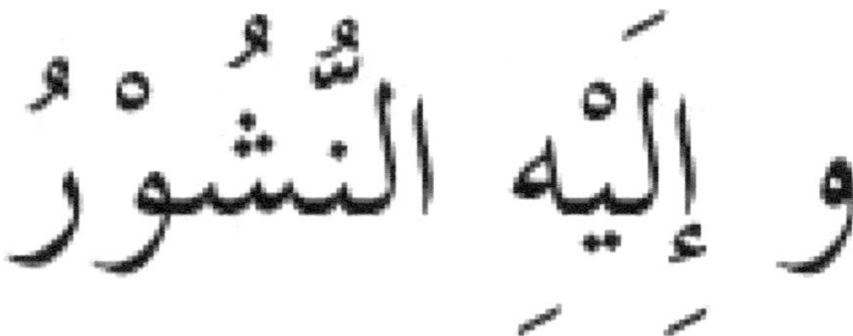

And to Him is the resurrection.

The Prophet (peace and blessings of Allah be upon him) said, '*Whoever awakes at night and then says*:

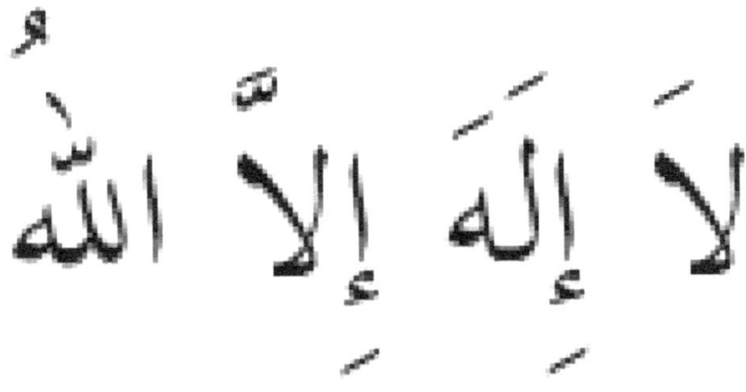

None has the right to be worshipped except Allah,

Alone without associate,

To him belongs sovereignty,

And to Him belongs praise,

And He -

عَلَى كُلِّ شَىْءٍ قَدِيرٌ.

- is over all things wholly capable.

How perfect is Allah,

and all praise is for Allah,

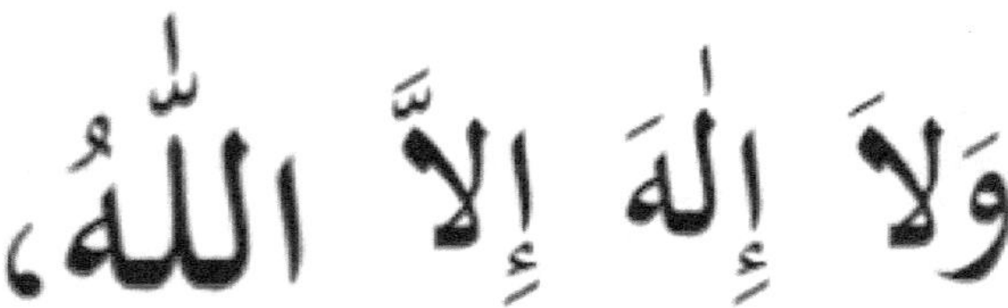

and none has the right to be worshipped except Allah,

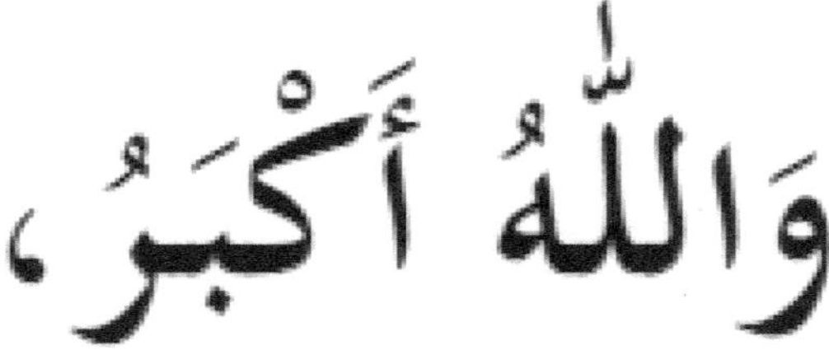

Allah is the Greatest.

And there is no power

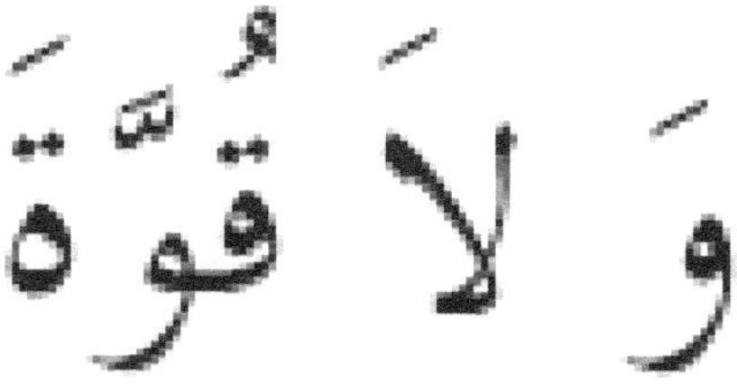

And there is no might -

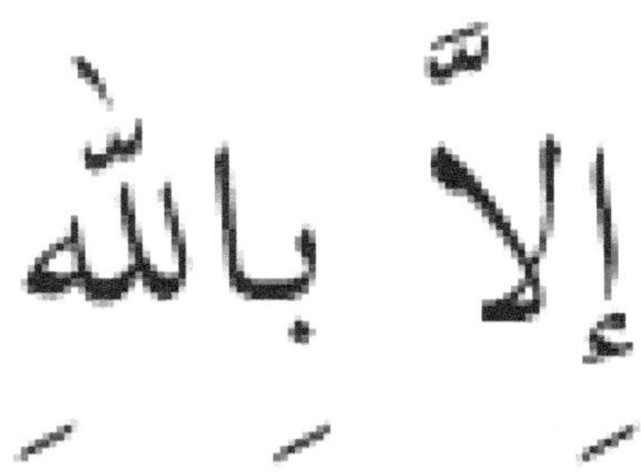

- except with Allah,

The Most High,

The Supreme.

The Prophet (peace be upon him) said, '*and then supplicates*:

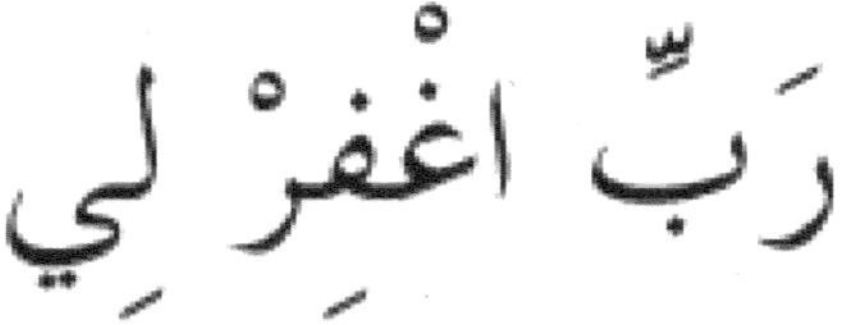

O my Lord forgive me.
… will be forgiven.'

Al-Waleed said, "or He (the Prophet, peace be upon him) said: '*and then asks, he will be answered. If he then performs ablution and prays, his prayer will be accepted*'."

<u>Prayer 3</u>

اَلْحَمْدُ لِلّٰهِ الَّذِي عَافَانِي فِي جَسَدِي

All praise is due to Allah Who healed me in my body,

and returned to me, my soul,

وَ أَذِنَ لِي بِذِكْرِه

and permitted me to remember him.

Before Entering The Toilet

In the name of Allah.

اَللّٰهُمَّ إِنِّي أَعُوذُ بِكَ

O Allah, I take refuge with You

مِنَ الْخُبُثِ وَالْخَبَائِثِ

from all evil and evil-doers.

The Messenger of Allah (peace and blessings of Allah be upon him) said: "The screen between the jinn and the nakedness of the children of Adam when they enter the lavatory is to say Bismillah."

When Starting

Ablution

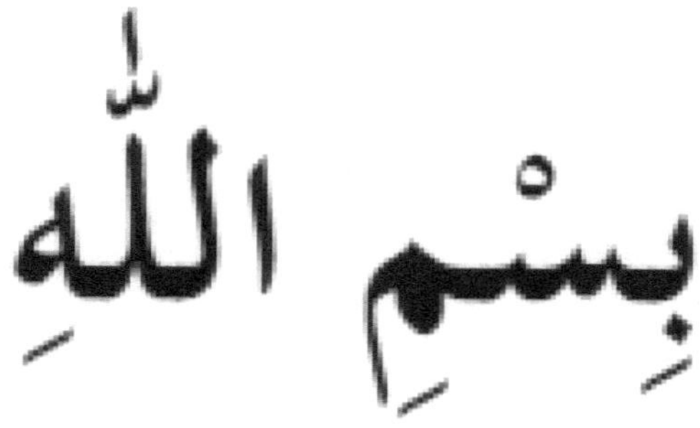

In the Name of Allah

After Completing

The Ablution

<u>Prayer 1</u>

أَشْهَدُ أَنْ لاَ إِلٰهَ إِلاَّ اللّٰهُ

I testify that there is none worthy of worship except Allah,

alone, without any partner,

وَأَشْهَدُ أَنَّ مُحَمَّدًا

and I testify that Muhammad

عَبْدُهُ وَرَسُولُهُ

is His servant and His Messenger.

The Messenger of Allah (peace and blessings of Allah be upon him) said: "Whoever perfects his

1

ablution (performs ablution and does it well), and then says [the above], the eight gates of Paradise will be opened for him. He may enter through whichever one he wishes."

PRAYER 2

سُبْحَانَكَ اللّٰهُمَّ وَبِحَمْدِكَ ،

You are free from imperfection, O Allah, and all
praise is to You,

أَشْهَدُ أَنْ لَّا إِلهَ إِلَّا أَنْتَ ،

I bear witness that there is no god but You,

أَسْتَغْفِرُكَ وَأَتُوبُ إِلَيْكَ.

I seek Your forgiveness and turn to You in
repentance.

The Messenger of Allah (peace and blessings of Allah be upon him) said: "Whosoever does ablution and says [the above], it will be recorded in a parchment and then sealed with a seal which will not be broken till the Day of Judgement."

After Leaving The Toilet

غُفْرَانَكَ

I ask You (Allah) for forgiveness

Before Removing Clothes

In the Name of Allah.

The Messenger of Allah (peace and blessings of Allah be upon him) said: 'The screen between the jinn and the nakedness of the children of Adam when they take off their garments is that they say Bismillah.'

After Wearing Clothes

اَلْحَمْدُ لِلّهِ الَّذِي

All praise is to Allah Who has –

كَسَانِي هَذَا الثَّوْبَ

- clothed me with this garment,

and provided me with it, without any power on my part

and without any might (on my part).

Allah has provided me with this garment without any power or might on my part.

The Messenger of Allah (peace and blessings of Allah be upon him) said: 'If anyone puts on a garment and says [the above], his past and future sins will be forgiven.'

After Wearing New Clothes

اَللّٰهُمَّ لَكَ الْحَمْدُ

O Allaah, for You is all praise.

أَنْتَ كَسَوْتَنِيهِ

You have clothed me with it.

أَسْأَلُكَ مِنْ خَيْرِهِ

I ask You for its good,

وَخَيْرِ مَا صُنِعَ لَهُ

and the good of which it was made,

وَأَعُوذُ بِكَ مِنْ شَرِّهِ

and I seek refuge in You from its evil,

وَشَرِّ مَا صُنِعَ لَهُ

and the evil for which it was made.

Supplication Said to Someone Who Is Wearing A New Garment

تُبْلِي وَيُخْلِفُ اللّٰهُ تَعَالَى

May you wear it out and Allah (Ta'aala) replace it (with another).

When Leaving The House

Prayer 1

بِسْمِ اللّٰهِ تَوَكَّلْتُ عَلَى اللّٰهِ

In the name of Allah, I have placed my trust in Allah.

لاَ حَوْلَ وَلاَ قُوَّةَ

There is no power (in averting evil) or strength (in attaining good) -

- except through Allah.

The Messenger of Allah (peace and blessings of Allah be upon him) said: "Whoever says [the above] when leaving his house will be told: 'You have been guided, you have been sufficed and you have been protected.' Then one devil says to another devil: 'How can you get to a man who has been guided, sufficed and protected?'"

O Allah! I seek refuge in You (seek your protection),

from misguiding others or being misguided;

from erring or others causing me to err;

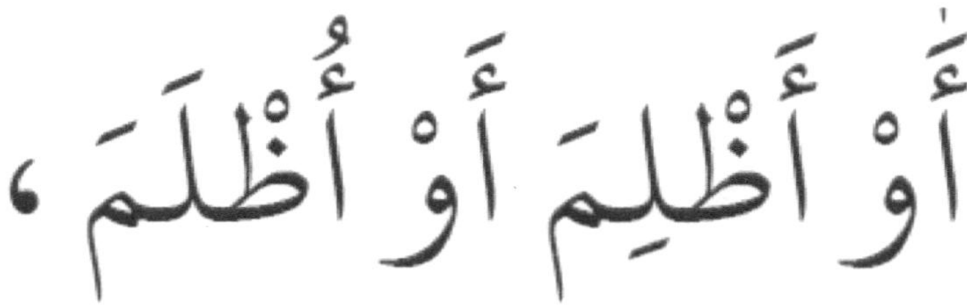

from oppressing others or being oppressed;

and from acting ignorantly or others acting
ignorantly towards me.

Umm Salamah said: "The Messenger of Allah
(peace and blessings of Allah be upon him) never
left my house without raising his eyes to the sky
and saying [the above].

When Entering The House

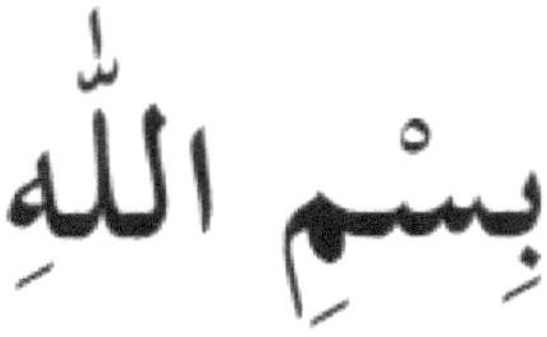

In the name of Allah.

The Messenger of Allah (peace and blessings of Allah be upon him) said: "When a man enters his house and remembers Allah upon entering and before eating, Shaytan says (to his fellow shaytān): 'There is no place for you to spend the night and there is no supper for you.' When he enters the house and does not remember Allah, Shaytān

says: 'You have found a place to spend the night.'
When he does not remember Allah before eating
his food, Shaytān says: 'You have found a place to
stay and some supper.'"

On The Way To The Mosque

اَللّٰهُمَّ اجْعَلْ فِيْ قَلْبِيْ نُوْرًا،

O Allah, place light in my heart,

وَفِيْ بَصَرِيْ نُوْرًا،

light in my sight,

وَفِي سَمْعِي نُوْرَاً،

and light in my hearing,

وَعَنْ يَمِيْنِي نُوْرًا،

and place light on my right,

وَعَنْ يَسَارِي نُوْرًا،

and place light on my left,

وَفَوْقِيْ نُوْرًا،

and place light above me,

and place light beneath me,

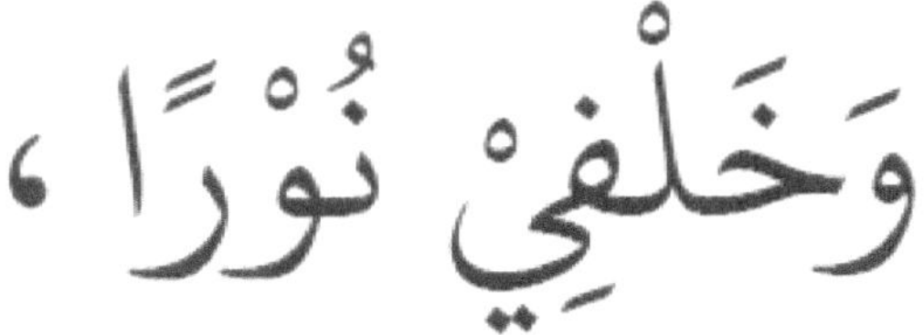

and place light in front of me,

and place light behind me,

وَاجْعَلْ لِّي نُوْرًا.

and grant me light.

When Entering The Mosque

أَعُوْذُ بِاللهِ الْعَظِيْمِ ،

I seek protection in Allah, the Supreme,

وَبِوَجْهِهِ الْكَرِيْمِ ،

by His Noble Face,

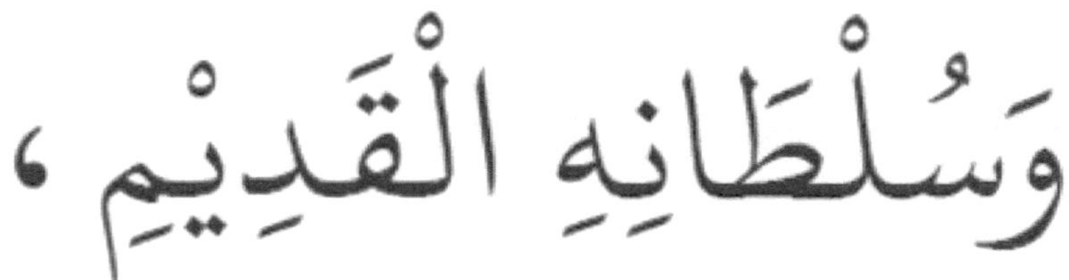

and His Eternal Authority

from the accursed Shaytan.

The Messenger of Allah (peace and blessings of Allah be upon him) said: "Whoever says [the above], Shaytān says: 'He has gained protection against me for the entire day.'"

When Leaving The

Mosque

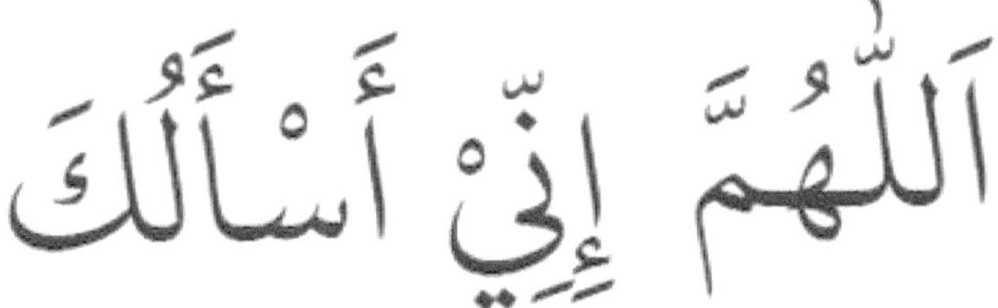

O Allah, I ask You

from Your Bounty.

Responding To the

Adhan

Prayer 1

Repeat the words of the mu'adhdhin, (except for)
"…when he says

Hasten to the prayer

and

Hasten to the salvation

Don't repeat these, instead, say:

لَا حَوْلَ وَلَا قُوَّةَ إِلَّا بِاللّه

There is no might and no power except by Allah

After the Adhan is complete say:

وَأَنَا أَشْهَدُ أَنْ لَا إِلٰهَ إِلَّا اللهُ

I also bear witness that there is no god but Allah.

وَحْدَهُ لَا شَرِيكَ لَهُ

And He is alone and He has no partner whatsoever,

وَ أَشْهَدُ أَنَّ

and I bear witness that

مُحَمَّداً عَبْدُهُ وَرَسُولُهُ،

Muhammad (peace and blessings of Allah be upon him) is His servant and His Messenger.

رَضِيتُ بِاللهِ رَبًّا،

I am satisfied with Allah as my Lord,

وَبِمُحَمَّدٍ رَسُولًا،

and with Muhammad as my Messenger,

and with Islam as my religion.

The Messenger of Allah (peace and blessings of Allah be upon him) said: "If anyone says [the above] on hearing the mu'adhdhin, his sins will be forgiven."

اَللّٰهُمَّ

O Allah,

رَبَّ هٰذِهِ الدَّعْوَةِ التَّامَّةِ

Lord of this perfect call –

وَالصَّلَاةِ الْقَائِمَةِ ،

and established prayer,

Grant

مُحَمَّدًا الْوَسِيْلَةَ وَالْفَضِيْلَةَ ،

Muhammad the status (a unique lofty status in Paradise) and pre-eminence,

وَابْعَثْهُ مَقَامًا مَّحْمُوْدًا الَّذِيْ

and resurrect him to the praiseworthy station that You have-

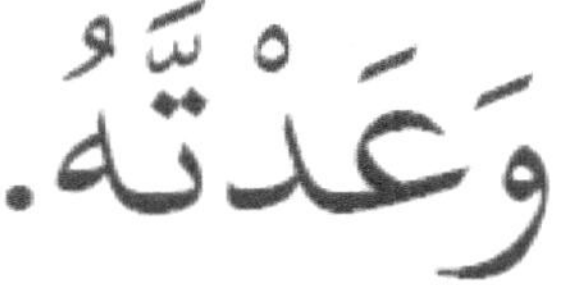

وَعَدْتَّهُ.

- promised him.

The Messenger of Allah (peace and blessings of Allah be upon him) said: "Whoever says [the above] after the adhān shall receive my intercession on the Day of Judgement."

The Messenger of Allah (peace and blessings of Allah be upon him) said: "Dua is not rejected between the adhan and the iqamah."

Dua For Isthikharah (Seeking Allah's Help In Making A Decision)

اَللّٰهُمَّ إِنِّيْ أَسْتَخِيْرُكَ

O Allah, I ask you for the best

through Your knowledge,

وَأَسْتَقْدِرُكَ بِقُدْرَتِكَ ،

I seek strength through Your power,

وَأَسْأَلُكَ مِنْ فَضْلِكَ الْعَظِيمِ ،

and I ask You from Your majestic benevolence.

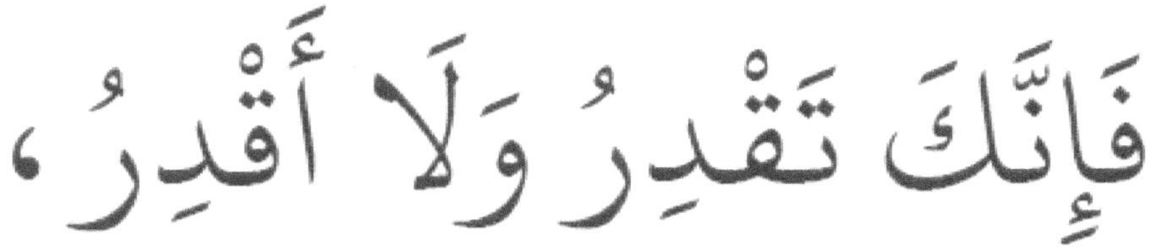

For You are fully able whilst I am not,

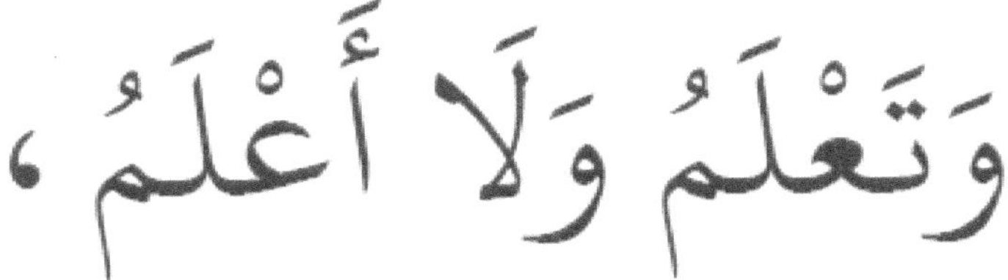

You know everything whilst I do not know anything,

and You are the Knower of the unseen.

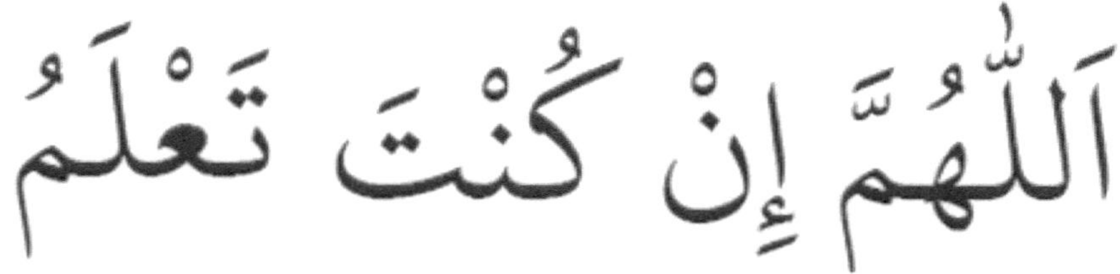

O Allah, if in Your knowledge,

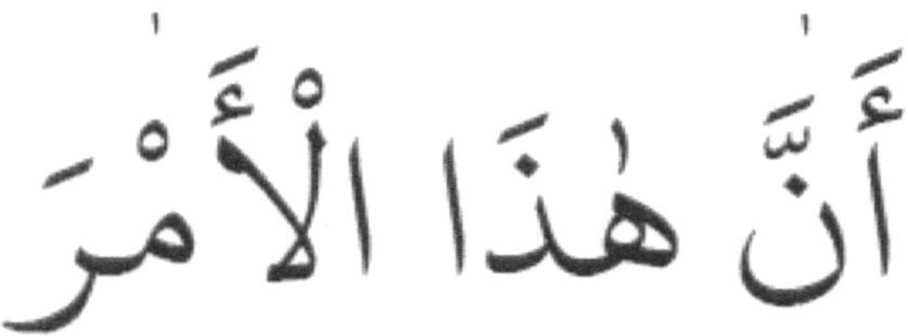

This matter

(وَيُسَمِّي حَاجَتَه)

(specify the matter and decision for which you are
seeking Allah's help now and then continue with
the Dua)

is good for me

in my religion,

my livelihood,

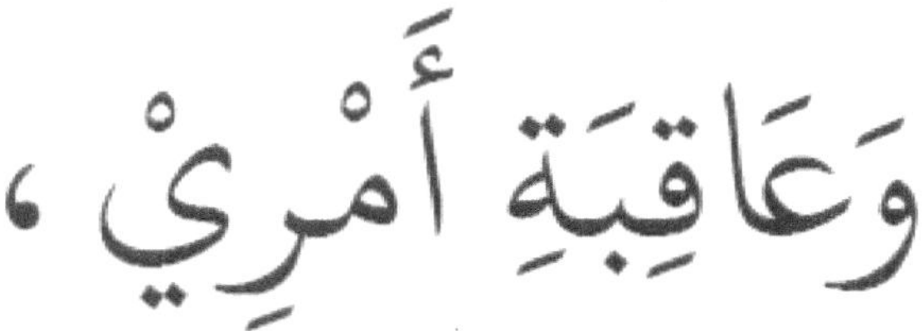

and my ultimate destiny,

then decree it for me,

and make it easy for me,

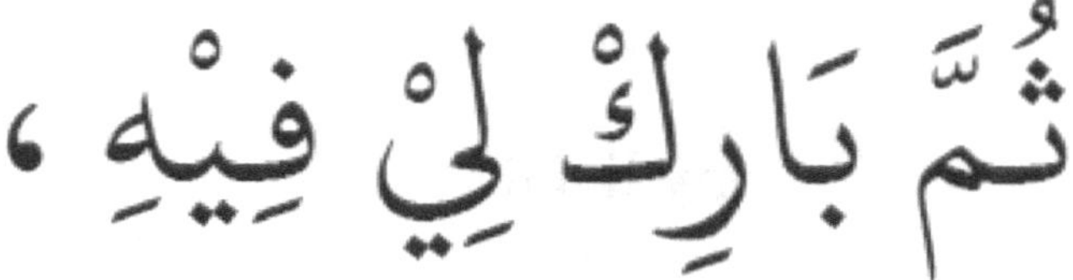

then bless it for me.

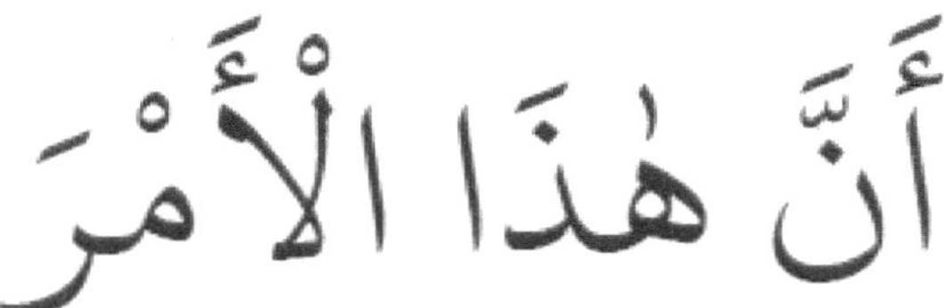

But if in your knowledge,

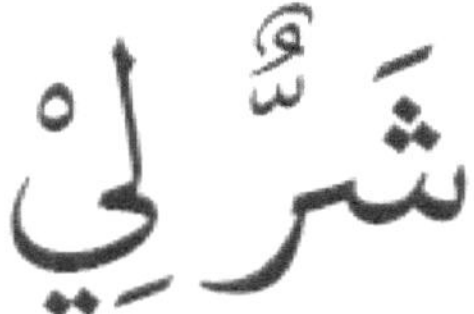

this matter

is bad for me

in my religion,

and my livelihood,

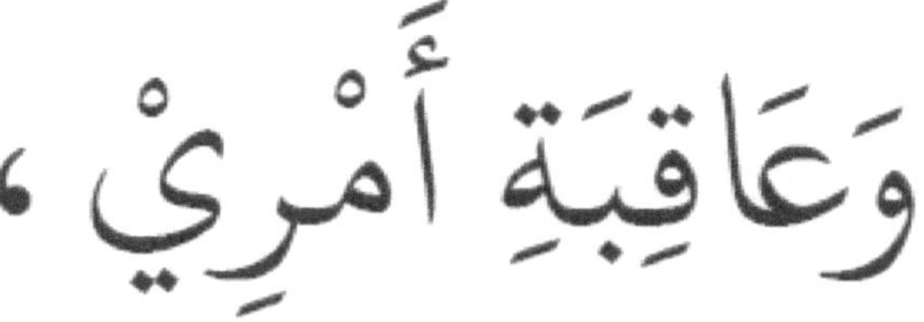

and my ultimate destiny,

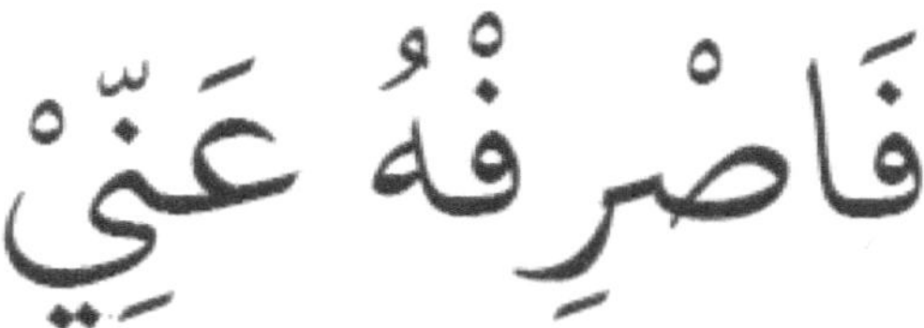

then turn it away from me,

and turn me away from it,

and decree good for me

wherever it may be,

then make me pleased with it.

Jabir narrated: "The Messenger of Allah (peace and blessings of Allah be upon him) used to teach us istikharah (when one seeks Allah's help in making a decision) for all matters, the same way he taught us Surahs from the Quran. He (peace and blessings of Allah be upon him) said: "When one of you intends to do something, he should offer two rak'ahs of voluntary Salah, and then say [the above]."

Before Eating

In the name of Allah.

If one forgets to say 'Bismillah' at the beginning
then he/she should say:

بِسْمِ اللهِ أَوَّلَهُ وَآخِرَهُ.

In the Name of Allah at the beginning and at the
end of it.

Umayyah said: "The Messenger of Allah (peace and blessings of Allah be upon him) was sitting whilst a man was eating food. That man did not mention the Name of Allah until only a morsel of food was left. When he raised it to his mouth, he said [the above]. The Messenger of Allah (peace and blessings of Allah be upon him) smiled at this and said: "Shaytaan had been eating with him but when he mentioned the Name of Allah, Shaytaan vomited all that was in his stomach."

After Eating

Praise be to Allah who has

fed me this,

and provided me with it

without any

power and might from me.

اَلْحَمْدُ لِلّٰهِ كَثِيرًا

Praise be to Allah with an abundant

طَيِّبًا مُبَارَكًا فِيهِ،

beautiful blessed praise,

غَيْرَ مَكْفِيٍّ،

a never-ending praise,

a praise which we will never bid farewell to,

and an indispensable praise.

رَبَّنَا

O our Lord!

After Opening A

Fast

The thirst has gone,

the veins have been moistened,

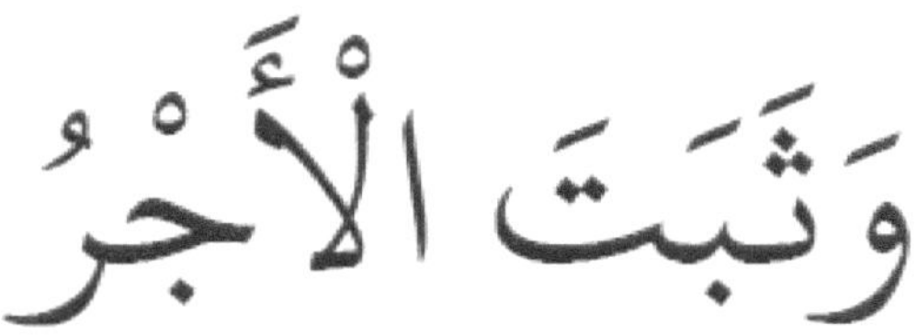

and the reward has been secured,

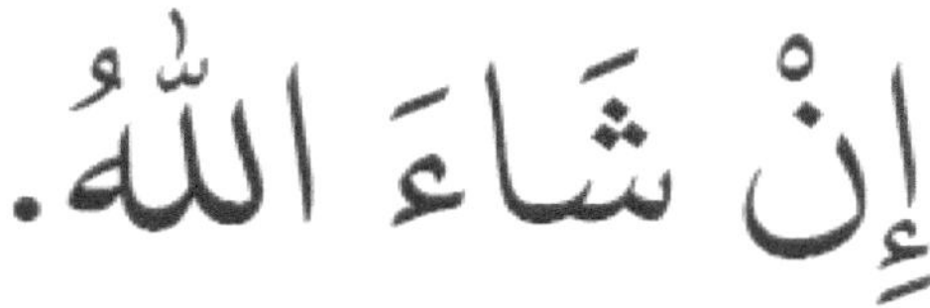

if Allah wills.

When It Rains

O Allah, make it a beneficial rain.

Upon Hearing Thunder

How perfect is the One Whom

the thunder exalts with praise of Him,

وَالْمَلَائِكَةُ مِنْ خِيْفَتِهِ.

as do the angels in awe of Him.

Seeking Allah's protection for children

I seek refuge for both of you

بِكَلِمَاتِ اللّٰهِ التَّامَّةِ

in the perfect words of Allah

from every devil

وَهَامَّةٍ

and every poisonous thing,

and from the evil eye which influences.

The Prophet (peace and blessings of Allah be upon him) used to entrust Hasan and Husayn in Allah's protection with the above words.

When Visiting The Sick

Prayer 1

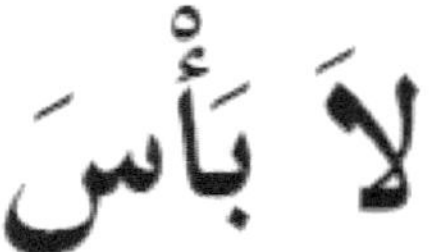

No worry,

It is purification,

إِنْ شَاءَ اللّهُ

If Allah wills.

I ask Allah, the Mighty,

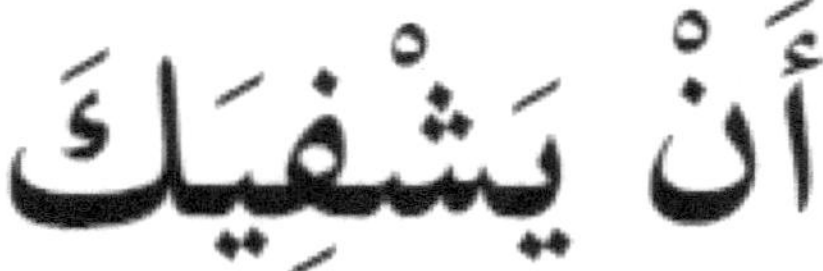

Lord of the mighty Throne,

أَنْ يَشْفِيَكَ

to heal you.

Read above Dua seven times.

The Messenger of Allah (peace and blessings of Allah be upon him) said: "He who visits a sick person who is not on the verge of death and supplicates [the above] seven times, Allah will certainly heal him from that sickness."

Supplication When Tragedy Strikes

We belong to Allah,

and to Him shall we

return;

O Allah, reward me

for my affliction,

and give me

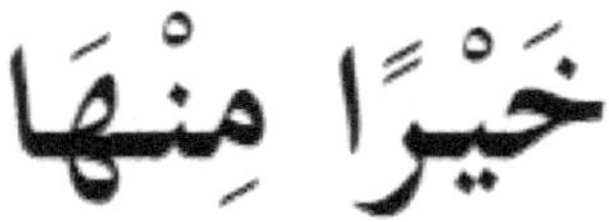

something better than it in its exchange.

What To Say When Consoling The Bereaved

إِنَّ لِلّٰهِ مَا أَخَذَ

Verily to Allah belongs what He took,

and to Him belongs what He gave,

and everything with Him

$$\text{بِأَجَلٍ مُسَمَّى}$$

has an appointed time.

After saying this Dua ask those grieving to have patience and hope for reward from Allah.

Dua When Sighting

The New Moon

اَللّٰهُمَّ أَهِلَّهُ عَلَيْنَا

O Allah, let the crescent loom above us

بِالْأَمْنِ

in safety,

and faith,

and peace,

and Islam.

My Lord,

وَرَبُّكَ

and your Lord

اللهُ

is Allah.

Dua By The Guest

For The Host

O Allah bless

them

in what You have provided them;

and forgive them,

وَارْحَمْهُمْ

and have mercy upon them.

Dua If Someone Gives You Food Or Drink

O Allah!

Feed him who fed me,

and give him drink who provided me drink.

Dua For The One Who Invites You To Break Your Fast With Them

أَفْطَرَ عِنْدَكُمُ الصَّائِمُونَ

May the fasting break their fast with you,

and the pious eat your food,

وَصَلَّتْ عَلَيْكُمُ الْمَلاَئِكَةُ

and the angels pray for blessing on you.

What Should A Fasting Person Say When Abused

I am fasting,

I am fasting.

Dua Upon Seeing The First Fruits Of The Season

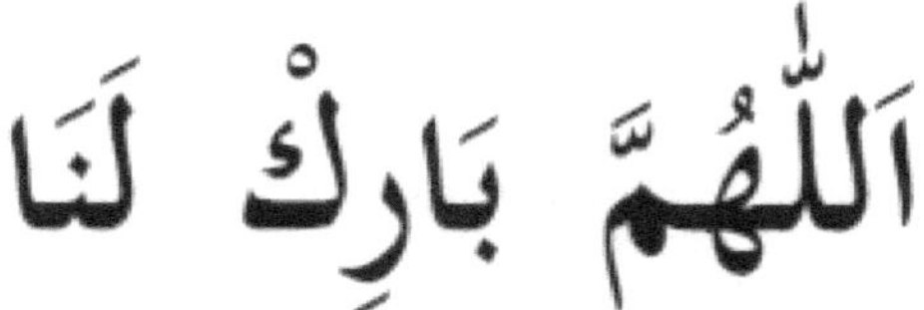

O Allah! Bless us

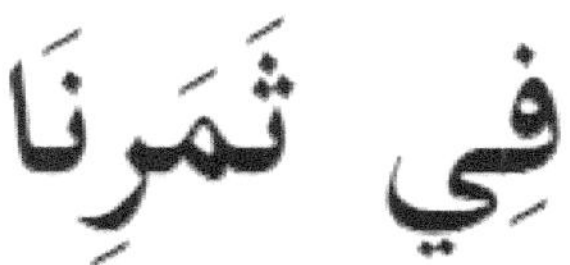

in our fruits;

and bless us in our city,

وَبَارِكْ لَنَا فِي صَاعِنَا

and bless us in our *saa* (a weighing unit),

وَبَارِكْ لَنَا فِي مُدِّنَا

and bless us in our *mudd* (a weighing unit).

Dua After Sneezing

Praise be to Allah.

Your companion who heard you sneezing and saying Alhamdulillaah, should say:

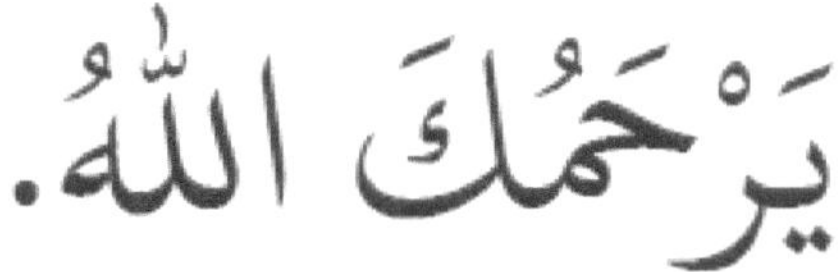

May Allah have mercy on you.

After this you should pray for him by saying:

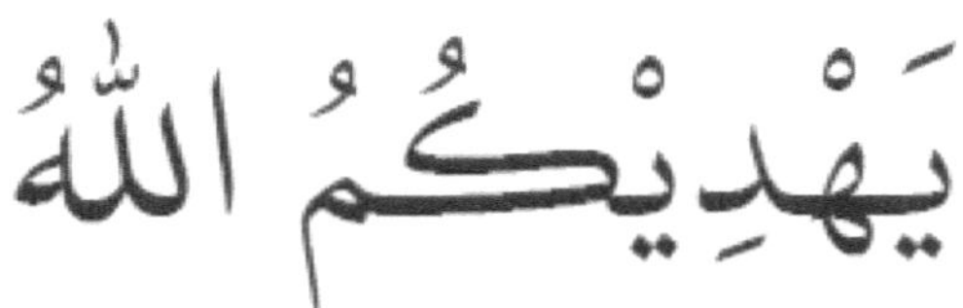

May Allah guide you,

and put your affairs in order.

For Firmness Of The Heart

يَا مُقَلِّبَ الْقُلُوْبِ

O Changer of the hearts,

ثَبِّتْ قَلْبِيْ عَلَىٰ دِيْنِكَ.

make my heart firm upon Your religion.

Anas said: "The Messenger of Allah (peace and blessings of Allah be upon him) would often say [the above]. So I asked: 'O Messenger of Allah, we believe in you and what you have come with, but do you fear for us?' He replied: 'Yes. Indeed the hearts are in between the two Fingers of Allah's Fingers. He changes them as He wills.'"

Dua To Congratulate Newly Weds

بَارَكَ اللّٰهُ لَكَ

May Allah bless for you,

وَبَارَكَ عَلَيْكَ

and may He bless on you,

and combine both of you in good.

Dua By The Groom For His Wife, And When Purchasing A New Ride

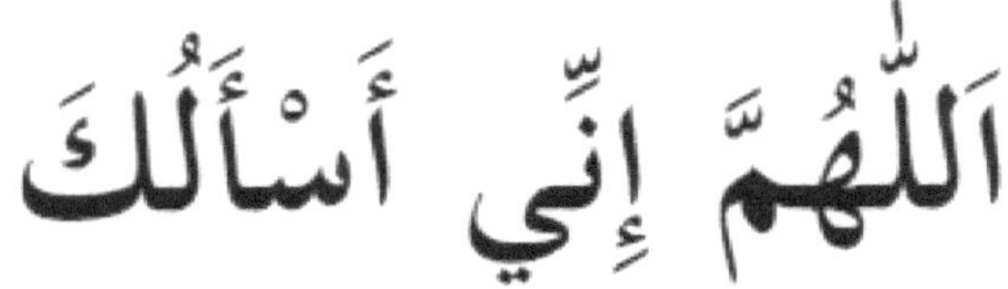

O Allah! I ask You

خَيْرَهَا

for the good in her,

وَخَيْرَ مَا جَبَلْتَهَا عَلَيْهِ

and the goodness that You have made her
inclined towards;

and I take refuge in You

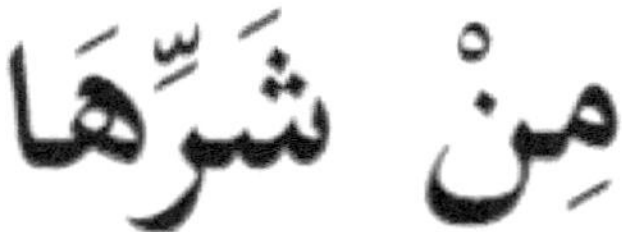

from the evil in her,

وَمِنْ شَرِّ مَا جَبَلْتَهَا عَلَيْهِ

and the evil that You have made her inclined towards.

Before Intercourse

بِسْمِ اللهِ اَللّٰهُمَّ

In the name of Allah, O Allah,

جَنِّبْنَا الشَّيْطَانَ

Protect us from Shaitaan,

وَجَنِّبِ الشَّيْطَانَ مَا رَزَقْتَنَا

and keep the shaitaan away from what you have
blessed us with (prevent shaitaan from
approaching our offspring).

Dua To Ward-off Anger

أَعُوذُ بِاللّٰهِ

I seek refuge in Allah

مِنَ الشَّيْطَانِ الرَّجِيمِ

from shaitaan the cursed one.

Dua On Seeing An Afflicted Person Or Upon Seeing Someone In Trial Or Tribulation

اَلْحَمْدُ لِلّٰهِ الَّذِي عَافَانِي

All praise is to Allah Who saved me

مِمَّا ابْتَلاَكَ بِهِ

from that which He has afflicted you with,

وَفَضَّلَنِي عَلَى كَثِيرٍ

and blessed me greatly over

مِمَّنْ خَلَقَ تَفْضِيلاً

much of His creation.

Dua While Sitting In A Gathering

O my Lord! Forgive me,

and accept my repentance.

إِنَّكَ أَنْتَ التَّوَّابُ الْغَفُورُ

Verily, You are the Oft-Returning, The Oft-Forgiving.

Supplication For The Expiation Of Sins Said After a Sitting or a Gathering

سُبْحَانَكَ اَللّٰهُمَّ وَبِحَمْدِكَ

How perfect You are O Allah, and I praise You,

أَشْهَدُ أَنْ لاَ إِلهَ إِلاَّ أَنتَ

I bear witness that there is none worthy of worship except You,

أَسْتَغْفِرُكَ وَأَتُوبُ إِلَيْكَ

I seek your forgiveness, and I repent to You.

Dua When Someone Seeks Forgiveness For You

When someone says:

غَفَرَ اللّٰهُ لَكَ

May Allah forgive you;

You should reply:

وَلَكَ

and you too.

Dua For The One Who Does You a Favour Or Who Does Good To You

جَزَاكَ اللّٰهُ خَيْرًا

May Allah give you a good reward.

Dua For The One Who Expresses His Love For Allah's Sake

When someone says:

I love you for Allah's sake;

You should reply to him by supplication for him the below words:

أَحَبَّكَ الَّذِي أَحْبَبْتَنِي لَهُ

May He for Whose sake you love me, love you.

Dua For The One Who Spends His Wealth On You

بَارَكَ اللّٰهُ لَكَ

May Allah bless you

فِي أَهْلِكَ وَمَالِكَ

in your family and wealth.

Dua When Repaying A Debt

بَارَكَ اللهُ لَكَ

May Allah bless you

فِي أَهْلِكَ وَمَالِكَ

in your family and wealth,

إِنَّمَا جَزَاءُ السَّلَفِ

the reward for lending

الْحَمْدُ

is praise

وَالأَدَاءُ

and repayment.

Dua For Protection

From Shirk

اَللّٰهُمَّ إِنِّي أَعُوذُ بِكَ

O Allah! I seek refuge with you

أَنْ أُشْرِكَ بِكَ

from associating anything with You

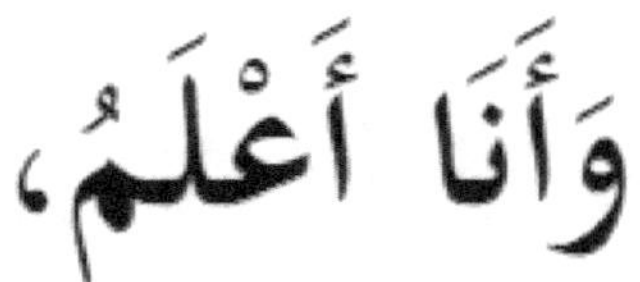

knowingly,

and I seek Your forgiveness

for that of which I am unaware.

Dua For The One Who Prays For Blessings For You

If someone prays for you by saying:

May Allah bless you

Then you should pray for him/her by saying:

And may Allah bless you (too).

Dua Against Superstition and forbiddance of ascribing things to omens

اَللّٰهُمَّ لَا طَيْرَ إِلَّا طَيْرُكَ،

O Allah, there is no omen but there is reliance on You,

وَلَا خَيْرَ إِلَّا خَيْرُكَ،

there is no good except Your good,

وَلَا إِلٰهَ غَيْرُكَ

and none has the right to be worshipped except You.

Duaa When Riding

A Vehicle Or An

Animal

بِسْمِ اللهِ وَ الْحَمْدُ لِلهِ،

In the name of Allah and all praise is for Allah,

سُبْحَانَ الَّذِي سَخَّرَ لَنَا هَذَا

How perfect He is, the One who has placed this
(transport) at our service,

وَمَا كُنَّا لَهُ مُقْرِنِينَ

and we ourselves would not have been capable of
that,

وَإِنَّا إِلَى رَبِّنَا لَمُنْقَلِبُونَ

and to our Lord is our final destiny.

اَلْحَمْدُ لِلّٰهِ اَلْحَمْدُ لِلّٰهِ
اَلْحَمْدُ لِلّٰهِ

All praise is for Allaah, All praise is for Allaah, All praise is for Allaah.

اَللّٰهُ أَكْبَرُ اَللّٰهُ أَكْبَرُ اَللّٰهُ أَكْبَرُ

Allaah is the Greatest, Allaah is the Greatest, Allaah is the Greatest.

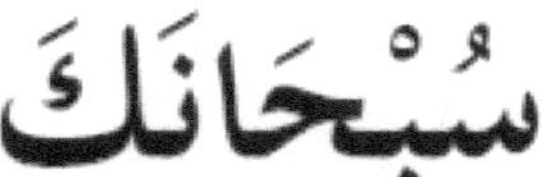

سُبْحَانَكَ

How perfect You are,

إِنِّي ظَلَمْتُ نَفْسِي

verily, I have wronged my soul,

so forgive me,

فَإِنَّهُ لاَ يَغْفِرُ الذُّنُوبَ إِلاَّ أَنْتَ

for surely none can forgive sins except You.

Dua At The Start Of A Journey And On Return

اَللهُ أَكْبَرُ اَللهُ أَكْبَرُ اَللهُ أَكْبَرُ

Allaah is the Greatest, Allaah is the Greatest,
Allaah is the Greatest,

سُبْحَانَ الَّذِي سَخَّرَ لَنَا هَذَا

How perfect He is, the One who has placed this
(transport) at our service,

وَمَا كُنَّا لَهُ مُقْرِنِينَ

and we ourselves would not have been capable of
that,

وَإِنَّا إِلَى رَبِّنَا لَمُنْقَلِبُونَ

and to our Lord is our final destiny.

اَللّٰهُمَّ إِنَّا نَسْأَلُكَ

O Allaah, we ask You for

فِي سَفَرِنَا هَذَا الْبِرَّ وَالتَّقْوٰى

birr and taqwa in this journey of ours,

وَمِنَ الْعَمَلِ مَا تَرْضٰى

and we ask You for deeds which please You.

اَللّٰهُمَّ هَوِّنْ عَلَيْنَا

O Allah, facilitate our

journey and let us cover its distance quickly.

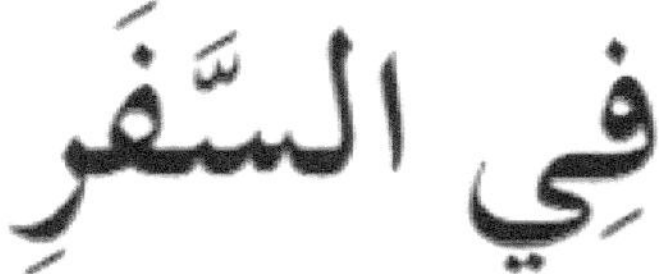

O Allah You are the Companion

on this journey

and The Successor (Guardian) over the family,

اَللّٰهُمَّ إِنِّي أَعُوذُ بِكَ

O Allah, I take refuge with You

مِنْ وَعْثَاءِ السَّفَرِ

from the difficulties (hardships) of travel (the journey),

وَكَآبَةِ الْمَنْظَرِ

gloominess of the sights,

وَسُوءِ الْمُنْقَلَبِ

and finding of evil changes

in property and family on return.

On returning, the Prophet (peace and blessings of
Allah be upon him) would recite the above dua,
and add the following:

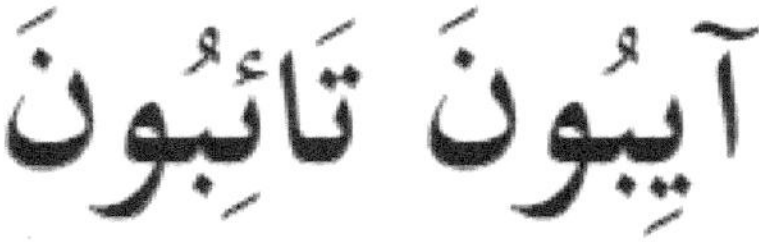

We return, repent,

worship, and praise our Lord.

Dua When Entering A Town Or City

اللَّهُمَّ رَبَّ السَّمَوَاتِ السَّبْعِ

O Allaah, Lord of the seven heavens

وَمَا أَظْلَلْنَ ،

and all that they envelop,

وَ رَبُّ الْأَرَاضِينَ السَّبْعِ

Lord of the seven earths

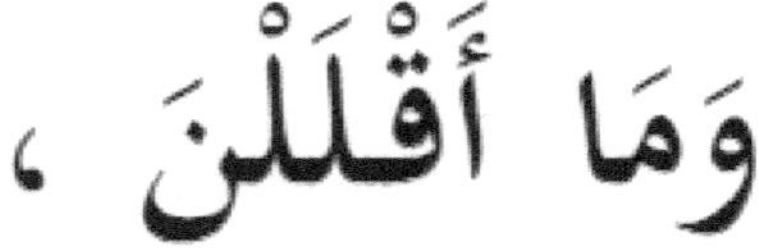

and all that they carry,

وَرَبُّ الشَّيَاطِينِ

Lord of the shaitaan (devils)

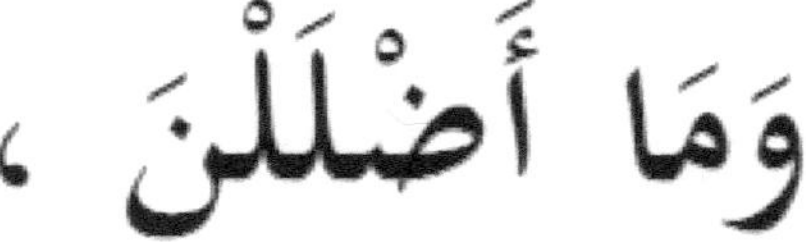

and all whom they misguide,

Lord of the winds

and all whom they whisk away,

I ask You

for the goodness of this village (town),

وَخَيْرَ أَهْلِهَا ،

the goodness of its inhabitants,

وَنَعُوذُ بِكَ

and we seek refuge with You

مِنْ شَرِّهَا وَشَرِّ أَهْلِهَا

from its evil, the evil of its people,

وَشَرِّ مَا فِيهَا

and the evil of what is in it.

لاَ إِلهَ إِلاَّ اللهُ وَحْدَهُ لاَ شَرِيكَ لَهُ

What to say when

entering a market

لاَ إِلٰهَ إِلاَّ اللّٰهُ وَحْدَهُ لاَ شَرِيكَ لَهُ

There is none worthy of worship except Allah,
Alone, without partner,

لَهُ الْمُلْكُ وَلَهُ الْحَمْدُ

to Him belongs the dominion, and to Him is all
the praise,

He gives life and causes death,

وَهُوَ حَيٌّ لاَ يَمُوتُ

He is Living and does not die,

بِيَدِهِ الْخَيْرُ

in His Hand is all the good,

وَ هُوَ عَلَى كُلِّ شَيْءٍ قَدِيرٌ

and He has power over all things.

Du'a For When Your Vehicle Or Mount Gives Trouble or Stumbles

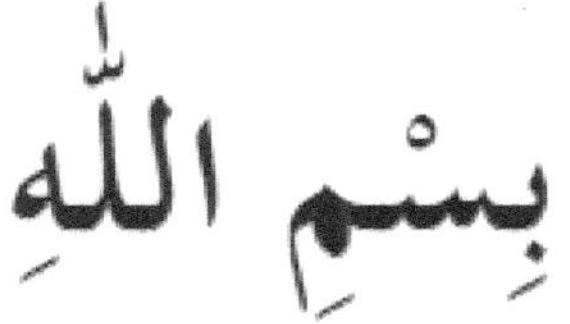

In the name of Allah.

Dua By The Traveler

For The Resident

أَسْتَوْدِعُكُمُ اللهَ الَّذِي

I leave you in the care of Allah Whose

لاَ تَضِيعُ وَدَائِعُهُ

trust is never lost.

The Morning And

The Evening Adhkar

Read the morning adhkar between Fajr and Sunrise

Read the evening adhkar between Asr and Maghrib

If you are not able to recite them during the above times, one can make up for them. For example, if you went back to sleep after Fajr then you can make up for them after waking up.

<u>Read both during morning and evening</u>

O Allah, We enter the morning by You

and we enter the evening by You.

وَبِكَ نَحْيَا،

We live by You

وَبِكَ نَمُوتُ،

and we die by You,

وَإِلَيْكَ النُّشُورُ

and to You is gathering (our resurrection).

<u>Read both during morning and evening</u>

اَللّٰهُمَّ أَنْتَ رَبِّي،

O Allah, You are my Lord,

لَا إِلٰهَ إِلاَّ أَنْتَ،

there is none worthy of worship but You,

خَلَقْتَنِي وَأَنَا عَبْدُكَ،

You created me and I am Your slave.

وَأَنَا عَلَى عَهْدِكَ

وَوَعْدِكَ مَا اسْتَطَعْتُ،

I keep Your covenant and my pledge to You so far
as I am able (as best as I can).

أَعُوذُ بِكَ مِنْ شَرِّ مَا صَنَعْتُ،

I seek refuge in You from the evil of what I have
done.

أَبُوءُ لَكَ بِنِعْمَتِكَ عَلَىَّ

I admit to Your blessings upon me,

وَأَبُوءُ لَكَ بِذَنْبِي،

and I admit to my sins,

فَاغْفِرْ لِي، فَإِنَّهُ لاَ يَغْفِرُ

Forgive me, for there is none

الذُّنُوبَ إِلاَّ أَنْتَ

who may forgive sins but You.

<u>Read below Dua 3 times both during morning and evening</u>

O Allah! Grant me health in my body.

O Allah! Grant me good hearing.

اَللّٰهُمَّ عَافِنِي فِي بَصَرِي

O Allah! Grant me good eyesight.

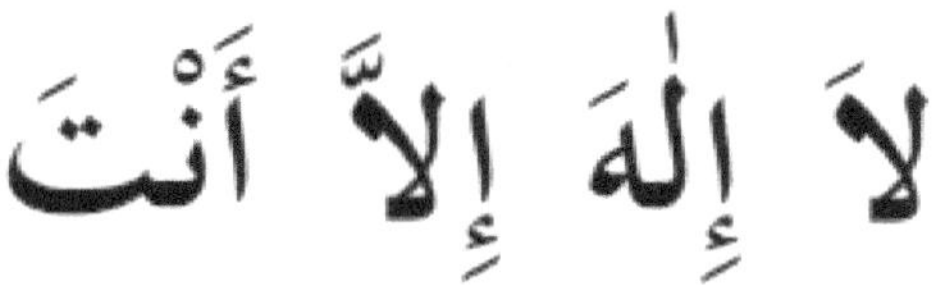

There is no god but You.

O Allah, I take refuge with You from disbelief

and poverty.

اَللّٰهُمَّ إِنِّي أَعُوذُ بِكَ مِنْ عَذَابِ الْقَبْرِ

O Allah! Verily, I seek refuge in You from the punishment in the grave.

لَا إِلٰهَ إِلاَّ أَنْتَ

There is no god but You.

Read below Dua three times both in the morning and in the evening

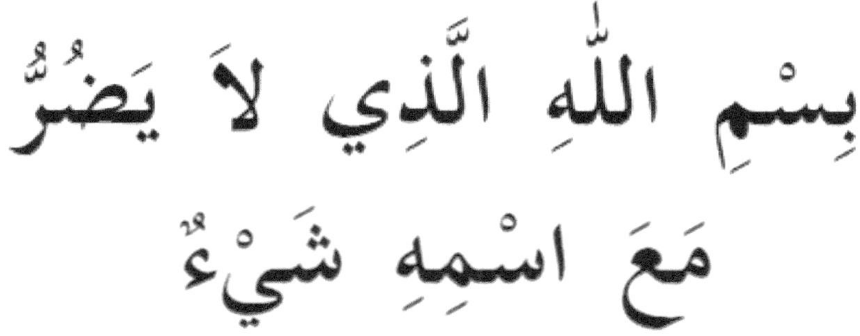

In the Name of Allah with whose name nothing is harmed

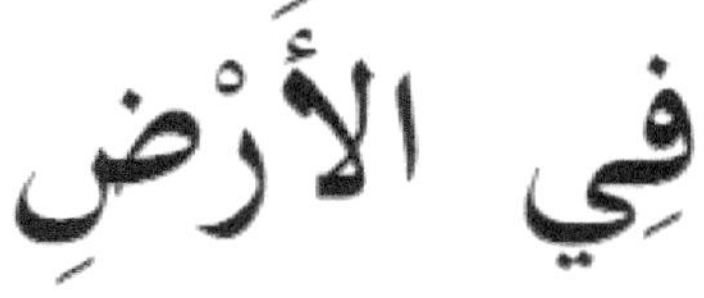

on earth

وَلاَ فِي السَّمَاءِ

nor in the heavens

and He is The All-Seeing, The All-Knowing.

by Your Mercy,

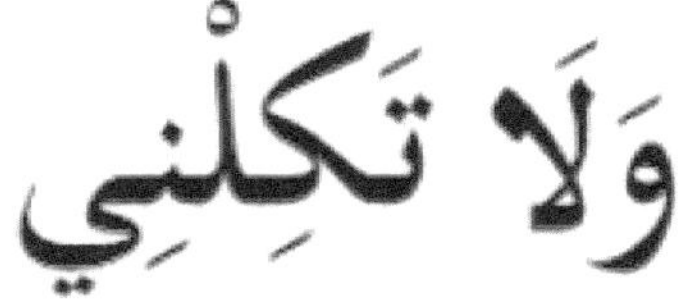

I call on You to set right all my affairs.

Do not place me

إِلَى نَفْسِي طَرْفَةَ عَيْنٍ

in charge of my soul even for the blinking of an
eye.

Ameen!